W9-BCQ-913

Mae Jemison

Trailblazing Astronaut, Doctor, and Teacher

Linda Barghoorn

Crabtree Publishing Company
www.crabtreebooks.com

Author: Linda Barghoorn

Series research and development: Reagan Miller

Editorial director: Kathy Middleton

Editor: Crystal Sikkens

Proofreader: Janine Deschenes

Photo researcher: Crystal Sikkens

Designer and prepress technician: Samara Parent

Print coordinator: Katherine Berti

Photographs:
AP Images: ©Mike Fisher: page 10; ©Bob Galbraith: page 14; ©Bob Gwaltney: page 16; ©Jim Cooper: page 25; ©PRNewsFoto/Bayer Corporation: page 26

Getty Images: ©Brendan Hoffman: pages 12-13; ©Gilbert Carrasquillo: page 17; ©Bettmann: page 19 (right); ©Afro Newspaper/Gado: page 21, 30; ©Lyn Alweis: page 27; ©Robert Mora: page 29

Keystone: ©NASA: page 22; ©Li Changxiang: page 28

Library of Congress: pages 6-7; page 15 (bottom left)

NASA: cover, title page, page 4; ©Neil A. Armstrong: page 8; ©Sheri Locke: page 20

Shutterstock: ©michael sheehan: page 9; ©360b (inset): page 11; ©jejim (bottom): page 11

Superstock: ©Everett Collection: page 23

Wikimedia Commons: ©Robert Prummel: page 15 (top right)

All other images from Shutterstock

Library and Archives Canada Cataloguing in Publication

Barghoorn, Linda, author
    Mae Jemison : trailblazing astronaut, doctor, and teacher / Linda Barghoorn.

(Remarkable lives revealed)
Includes index.
Issued in print and electronic formats.
ISBN 978-0-7787-2693-7 (hardback).--
ISBN 978-0-7787-2704-0 (paperback).--ISBN 978-1-4271-1814-1 (html)

    1. Jemison, Mae, 1956- --Juvenile literature. 2. African American women astronauts--Biography--Juvenile literature. 3. Women astronauts--United States--Biography--Juvenile literature. 4. Astronauts--United States--Biography--Juvenile literature. 5. Manned space flight--Juvenile literature. I. Title.

TL789.85.J46B37 2016   j629.450092   C2016-904115-8
                                          C2016-904116-6

Library of Congress Cataloging-in-Publication Data

Names: Barghoorn, Linda, author.
Title: Mae Jemison : trailblazing astronaut, doctor, and teacher / Linda Barghoorn.
Description: St. Catharines, Ontario ; New York, NY : Crabtree Publishing Company, [2016] | Series: Remarkable lives revealed Includes index.
Identifiers: LCCN 2016026665 (print) | LCCN 2016027154 (ebook) | ISBN 9780778726937 (reinforced library binding) | ISBN 9780778727040 (pbk.) | ISBN 9781427118141 (Electronic HTML)
Subjects: LCSH: Jemison, Mae, 1956---Juvenile literature. | African American women astronauts--Biography--Juvenile literature. | Women astronauts--United States--Biography--Juvenile literature. | Astronauts--United States--Biography--Juvenile literature. | Manned space flight--Juvenile literature.
Classification: LCC TL789.85.J46 B37 2016 (print) | LCC TL789.85.J46 (ebook) | DDC 629.45/0092 [B] --dc23
LC record available at https://lccn.loc.gov/2016026665

Crabtree Publishing Company

www.crabtreebooks.com   1-800-387-7650

Printed in Canada/082016/TL20160715

Published in Canada
Crabtree Publishing
616 Welland Ave.
St. Catharines, Ontario
L2M 5V6

Published in the United States
Crabtree Publishing
PMB 59051
350 Fifth Ave., 59th Floor
New York, NY 10118

Published in the United Kingdom
Crabtree Publishing
Maritime House
Basin Road North, Hove
BN41 1WR

Published in Australia
Crabtree Publishing
3 Charles Street
Coburg North
VIC, 3058

Contents

Space Dreams

Every person's life is a collection of stories about their experiences. Stories about remarkable people, even if they are not well known, can inspire us as we think about our own lives. What makes someone remarkable? Maybe it is their bravery, imagination, or intelligence. Everyone has a different idea of what makes someone remarkable. As a child, Mae Jemison (*JEH-mih-sun*) loved to stare at the stars and dreamed of traveling to Mars. She grew up to follow those dreams right into space!

What is a Biography?

A biography is the story of a person's life. We read biographies to learn about a person's experiences and thoughts. Biographies can be based on many sources of information. Primary sources include a person's own words or pictures. Secondary sources include stories from friends, family, media, and research.

As you read Mae's story, think about the qualities she has that helped her achieve her dream.

Bold and Pioneering

Mae Jemison is passionate about science and learning. In kindergarten she knew she wanted to be a scientist. As a young African American, she faced many **racial barriers** to achieving her dreams. But she refused to be limited by other people's ideas. She is determined, daring, and confident.

? THINK ABOUT IT

Do you know someone who is remarkable? What qualities do they have that you find remarkable?

*Mae's work is bold and **pioneering**. It inspires others to reach for their own dreams.*

Chapter 1

Reaching for the Stars

Mae Jemison was born in Alabama in 1956. She is the youngest of three children. Her father was a carpenter and her mother was a teacher. Her family moved to Chicago when Mae was three to find better opportunities for education. Mae's parents encouraged their children's individual talents and dreams. They taught them to believe in themselves and their rights as African Americans.

Equal Rights

Segregation was still practiced when Mae was a child. This meant that African Americans were sometimes kept separate from other Americans. They could not always use the same restaurants, bathrooms, buses, and schools. They did not have the same career opportunities. During the Civil Rights Movement there were many protests by African Americans to change this. As Mae grew older she understood that she deserved the same rights to pursue her dreams as every American.

Civil Rights Movement

In the 1950's and 1960's, African Americans began to protest segregation. This became known as the Civil Rights Movement. Its goal was to provide equal rights to everyone regardless of their race, gender, or religion. In 1964, the United States president signed a law to ban segregation.

Civil rights protestors march from Selma to Montgomery, Alabama in 1965.

Fascinated by Space

Mae was a curious, imaginative child who was eager to learn. She loved to read and enjoyed books about the universe. Her favorite books featured female scientists and **heroines**. She also loved science and space. Mae eagerly watched the Apollo space missions on television. She imagined what it would be like to travel into space herself. This became her dream.

> Growing up I always assumed I would go into space.
>
> —Mae Jemison. Makers Profile: Mae Jemison

The Apollo space missions aimed to land humans on the moon. Buzz Aldrin, an American astronaut, places a flag to celebrate the first moon landing on July 20, 1969.

A Love of Dance

Mae's curiosity and energy led her to explore many subjects. In eighth grade she convinced her mother to enroll her in dance classes. She loved dance because it gave her a chance to be creative. She trained in different dance styles such as ballet, jazz, and African dance. Dancing helped her improve her coordination and physical strength. It also taught her the importance of practice and hard work to achieve her goals. And, dance gave her the confidence to perform in front of others. Mae has continued to dance her whole life.

? THINK ABOUT IT

Why was dance important to Mae? What did it teach her?

African dance celebrates the life and culture of a community. Above, dancers and musicians in South Africa perform for tourists.

Arts and Science

Mae loves both the arts and science. She insists they are equally important to help us build a better world. She believes science helps us better understand the physical world around us. We can use science to continue to improve our lives on Earth. The arts let us share our unique and personal views of the world with others. This gives us many different and exciting ways of looking at the world, as well as many ways to share it effectively with each other.

> *The arts and the sciences provide a fuller understanding of the universe around us.*
>
> —**Mae Jemison. PBS: The Secret Life of Scientists and Engineers, The Cosmic Dance interview, 2016.**

Mae attended Morgan Park High School as a teenager. She joined school principal Earl Bryant in a ceremony in 1992 to honor her achievements.

University at Sixteen

When she was just 16, Mae Jemison received a scholarship to Stanford University in California. Following her love for science and art, she studied Chemical Engineering and African American studies. She also learned to speak Russian, Japanese, and **Swahili** (*swah-HEE-lee*), and took part in dance and theater productions. While at university, she realized that women and **minorities** were not given the same opportunities to enroll and be successful in science programs. Mae felt strongly that this needed to change.

Chemical Engineering

Chemical engineering uses science to solve real world challenges by turning chemicals into useful things.

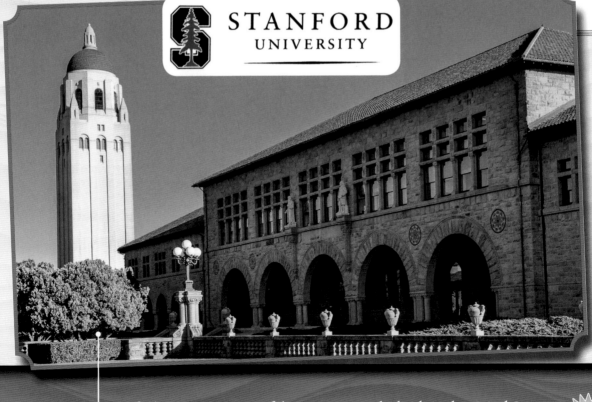

STANFORD UNIVERSITY

Stanford University is one of the most respected schools in the United States.

Chasing a Dream

When she was a young girl, Mae was often told she couldn't pursue her dreams of traveling to space. Some people believed women and minorities didn't have the necessary skills and intelligence to pursue challenging careers. In the 1960s, few women became scientists, and even fewer were African American. Women were encouraged to pursue careers in only a limited number of fields such as nursing and teaching.

? THINK ABOUT IT

What was one of the biggest challenges Mae faced in pursuing her space career?

> *Never be limited by other people's limited imaginations.*
>
> —Mae Jemison, Annual Biomedical Research Conference for Students, 2009

Overcoming Barriers

People suggested that Mae should pursue a career more suitable for a girl. They were surprised by her determination to be a scientist. Mae's intelligence and confidence in her abilities helped her to believe in herself. She refused to let anyone stand in the way of her dreams. As she grew older, she continued to challenge barriers for women and minorities. She has been a strong supporter for equal rights throughout her career.

Mae Jemison participates in a program where successful women talk with high school students about achieving their dreams.

Role Models

Mae Jemison was inspired by many people as she took bold steps to follow her dreams. Her parents, family, friends, and teachers all played a part in her success. They taught her about strength of character and personal values. They encouraged her to always believe in herself and to stand up for change.

Her mother inspired her belief in the importance of education and lifelong learning. She challenged Mae to take risks to reach her greatest potential and follow her dreams.

? THINK ABOUT IT

Who were Mae's role models as she grew up? How did they influence her?

A Science Hero

One of Mae's heroes was Linus Pauling (*PAW-lihng*), a great scientist and **humanitarian**. He won the Nobel Prize for Chemistry in 1954 and for Peace in 1962. He was the only person ever to receive two Nobel prizes on his own. Mr. Pauling was a dedicated and knowledgeable scientist. He was also committed to help improve the lives of others and he used science to do this.

Nobel Prize

Nobel Prizes are awarded each year to people who have done outstanding work in Physics, Chemistry, Medicine, Literature, Economics or Peace.

Linus Pauling inspired Mae to use science to help improve humanity.

Incredible Women

As a child, Mae didn't know about the incredible roles women had played in aviation and **aerospace**. She didn't think about what it would mean to be the first African American woman to travel to space. She just wanted to go to space. When she finally accomplished her goal, she realized she could be a role model for others. She believes it's important for women to support one another to achieve their goals.

> It's important…for a little black girl growing up to know, yeah, you can become an astronaut because here's Mae Jemison.
>
> —Mae Jemison, New York Times 'Woman in the News: A determined breaker of Boundaries – Mae Carol Jemison', 1992

An elementary student holds a picture of Mae Jemison as she celebrates African American History Month at school.

Rules for Success

Mae follows four rules for success:

1. Learn from fear. Push yourself to do things you're afraid of and try new things. This will make you stronger, more confident, and teach you new skills.

2. Help each other make a difference. Celebrate your successes to show others why they should also pursue their dreams.

3. Eliminate **prejudice**. Don't allow yourself to be limited by other people's opinions of what you can achieve.

4. Be **inclusive**. Include people of all genders, races, and religions to work closely with one another to build a better society.

Mae Jemison attends a "Celebration of American Women" at Drexel University in Philadelphia.

The Road to NASA

In 1977, Mae graduated from Stanford with a Bachelor of Science degree. Now she had to choose whether to pursue a career in science or professional dance. She decided to study medicine and was accepted to Cornell University Medical College. While she was there, she decided she wanted to learn more about the world. So she decided to study abroad in Cuba and Kenya. She also worked at a **refugee camp** in Thailand.

Dr. Mae

In 1981, Mae received her medical degree and began work as a doctor. She then traveled to West Africa as a medical officer with the Peace Corps. The Peace Corps is an organization that sends volunteers to underdeveloped countries to help with health, education, industry, and farming. Mae spent several years doing research in Sierra Leone and Liberia.

> Life is full of adventures. Some of them will be more demanding than others, but they all teach us about the world and ourselves along the way. Learn from your experiences—they shape who you become.
>
> —Mae Jemison. Black History Month: Mae Jemison, Persephone Magazine, 2011.

NORTH
PACIFIC

THAILAND

AUSTRALIA

Dr. Jemison in her office in Los Angeles. She worked as a doctor in the U.S. before joining the Peace Corps in Africa.

19

Becoming an Astronaut

Mae was always looking for new challenges. So in 1987, she decided to apply to **NASA**'s astronaut training program. Almost 200 people applied to the program. Mae was one of only 15 people chosen. She was the first female African American to be accepted. She thanks people like Morgan Watson and Walter Applewhite with helping to break down racial barriers at NASA. They were some of the first African American scientists to work at NASA several decades earlier.

The Johnson Space Center is in Houston, Texas. It is the main center for space flight training and research in America.

> I called down to Johnson Space Center. I said I would like an application to be an astronaut. They didn't laugh!
>
> —Mae Jemison. PBS: The Secret Life of Scientists and Engineers, I Wanted to Go Into Space interview, 2016.

NASA and Equal Rights

Dr. Jemison is proud of NASA's role in advancing equal rights for women and people of all races. As NASA was building its space program in the 1960s it hired the best scientists in the country, regardless of their race or gender. NASA took a leading role to give people of all races the same rights and opportunities for careers. This helped lead the way for Mae.

Dr. Mae Jemison becomes the first African American female astronaut in 1991.

21

Mae in Space

After more than a year of training, Mae's lifelong dream of traveling to space finally came true. In September 1992, she became the first African American woman in space. She joined six other astronauts aboard the Space Shuttle Endeavour's STS-47 Spacelab-J mission. Mae conducted scientific experiments on weightlessness and motion sickness on the space shuttle's crew. The mission lasted eight days and Mae logged over three million miles orbiting Earth. She even danced while in space!

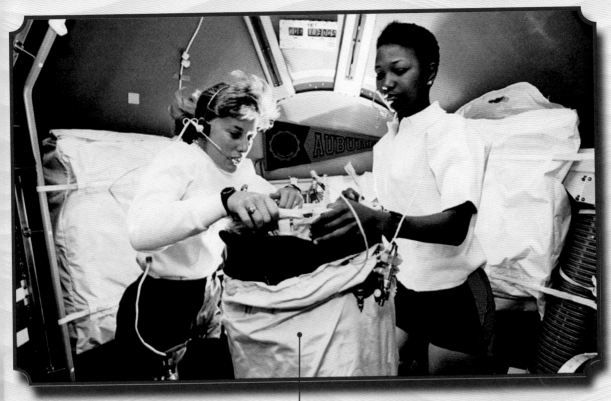

Doctors Jan Davis and Mae Jemison conduct gravity tests aboard the Space Shuttle Endeavour.

Mae's Space Kit

As Mae prepared for space travel, she felt it was important to take things into space that represented her African American heritage. When she was growing up, the achievements of African American people weren't always celebrated. To change this, she packed a poster of Judith Jamison, an African American ballet dancer; a Bundu statue from the women's society in West Africa; and a flag from Alpha Kappa Alpha—the oldest African American women's sorority, or organization of female college students, in the United States. This was Mae's way of celebrating her achievement as an African American female and sharing it with others.

Advancing Science and Space Exploration

The Jemison Group consults on the design and implementation of solar power systems like these in Africa.

Science and Society

In 1993, Dr Jemison left the NASA program. She created the Jemison Group in 1994 to continue her work using science in our everyday lives. Her company researches, develops, and markets technologies to help improve the lives of people around the world. One of the group's projects consults on the design and installation of solar power systems in developing countries. Another project uses satellite-based **telecommunications** to help deliver health care in remote areas of Africa. They also work to develop medical products using NASA technology.

Excellence in Education

Mae, along with her brother and sister, created the Dorothy Jemison Foundation for Excellence in honor of their mother Dorothy Jemison. Dorothy always inspired a high standard for personal excellence in Mae and always pushed Mae to become better. This organization develops teaching materials and programs to improve education around the world. Its aim is to inspire individuals to achieve excellence as they reach for their personal goals. Mae believes that each person can—and should—be expected to make a unique contribution to society.

Dr. Jemison serves as Bayer Corporation's national science literacy advocate.

Space Camp

As part of the Dorothy Jemison Foundation for Excellence, Mae created The Earth We Share international space camp. It brings students from the ages of 12 to 16 together from around the world to solve global problems. They discuss issues such as, "How many people can Earth hold?" or "Should we try to develop a weather machine?" Students learn how science connects to everyday life. They also learn what kinds of careers are available in science and technology, and how their own skills and interests might fit in these jobs.

Along with her international space camp program, Mae works with other camps across America to help students learn science.

Space cam

Many kids love science and have a natural curiosity about the world. They ask questions such as, "Why is the sky blue?" and "Why do I need to breathe?" Mae believes we need to do a better job to keep students interested in science as they grow up because science is so important to the health of our planet. It shapes the way we grow our food, the kinds of cars we drive, and the homes we live in. By keeping students engaged with science, we will improve their science literacy, or knowledge and ability. This will help them make better decisions as we work to improve life on Earth.

THINK ABOUT IT

Why is science literacy so important to Dr. Jemison?

Mae Jemison helps a teenage hospital patient conduct a science experiment.

100 Year Starship Project

Dr. Jemison created the 100 Year Starship project to plan the next steps of **interstellar** travel. She hopes to get humans to travel beyond our solar system in the next 100 years and to use research to improve the quality of life on Earth. In April 2016, Mae was part of a team of scientists and businesspeople that announced the Breakthrough Starshot Project. This project aims to send many tiny robotic spacecraft to the nearest star system to Earth to collect data. New technology will need to be developed to help the spacecraft travel up to 100 million miles per hour (160 million kilometers per hour). This speed would get them to the star system in just 20 years, rather than 78,000 years using current technology.

Dr. Jemison speaks at the "Starshot" project press conference in New York.

What's Next?

Daring and accomplished, Mae Jemison is one of the most admired women in the world. She has served on numerous boards and committees and has won countless honors and awards, including earning a place in the National Women's Hall of Fame and International Space Hall of Fame. She has become a doctor, scientist, professor, astronaut, TV star, and role model. It's hard to say what great things Mae will accomplish next—the sky's the limit!

Mae became the first real astronaut ever to appear on the TV series Star Trek: The Next Generation. *She is shown here at the world premiere of the movie* Star Trek: Nemesis.

Writing Prompts

1. What personal characteristics do you believe are important to achieve your dreams? Which of these did you see in Mae?

2. What do you believe is Mae's greatest accomplishment? Why?

3. Why does Mae Jemison believe art and science are equally important in helping us achieve a better world?

4. How has Dr. Jemison used her remarkable career to help empower others?

5. Has Dr. Mae's story inspired you to follow your dreams? How?

6. Do you agree with Mae's "Rules for Success"? Do you have any of your own to add?

7. What do you think Mae Jemison means when she says "we're all on this spaceship Earth"?

Learning More

Books

The 100 Year Starship: Astronaut Dr Mae Jemison. Jemison, Mae, Rau, Meachen. Scholastic. 2013

Women in Space. Caitlin McAneney. Powerkids Press. 2015

Journey Through our Solar System. Mae Jemison. Scholastic. 2013

The Everything Kids' Astronomy Book. Kathi Wagner, Sheryl Racine. Adams Media. 2008

Find Where The Wind Goes: Moments From My Life. Dr. Mae Jemison. Scholastic Press. 2001

Websites

www.esa.int/esaKIDSen/
Fun interactive website for kids to explore facts about earth, our universe, life in space and technology.

http://blackhistorycanada.ca
People and events that have shaped black history in Canada.

http://teacher.scholastic.com/space/mae%5Fjemison/interview.htm
Interview with Dr Mae Jemison.

www.greatblackheroes.com
A look at black heroes throughout history.

http://teacher.scholastic.com/activities/women/notable.htm
An honor roll of important and pioneering women.

Glossary

aerospace The industry that deals with travel in and above Earth's atmosphere

heroine A female who is admired for her bravery or character

humanitarian A person who works to make other people's lives better

inclusive Including everything or everyone

interstellar Existing or occurring between stars

minority A small group of people with a different religion, race, or gender than the larger group

NASA Short for National Aeronautics and Space Administration, it is the U.S. government agency responsible for space exploration and research.

pioneering Using new or creative ideas to solve a problem or challenge

prejudice An unfair feeling of dislike for someone because of their race, gender, or religion

racial barrier A rule that makes it difficult for people of a different race to succeed

refugee camp A place where people forced to leave their countries to find safety stay before finding a permanent home

segregration A policy that keeps people of different races or religions separate from each other

Swahili An East African language

telecommunications The technology of sending and receiving signals and images over long distances by telephone, television, or satellite

Index